NATIONAL GEOGRAPHIC **OUR WORLD**

The Three Bears

A fairy tale
Retold by Tom Davison

NATIONAL
GEOGRAPHIC
L E A R N I N G

The three bears leave their house.

Goldilocks comes in.

Goldilocks is in the kitchen.
She's eating Baby Bear's food!

Now she's in the living room.
She's breaking Baby Bear's chair!

Now Goldilocks is in the bedroom.
She's sleeping in Baby Bear's bed!

The three bears come home.
Baby Bear says, 'Where is my food?'

'Where is my chair?' says Baby Bear.

'Who is sleeping in my bed?'

Goldilocks runs away!

The three bears never see
Goldilocks again.

Facts About Bears

Some bears find special homes for the winter. These homes are called dens. Bears sleep in their dens for months without eating!

under a tree

in a cave

under a rock

Some bears dig dens in snow. They do not go into dens just to sleep. They go into dens to have babies!

Fun with Homes

Where do you do it? Circle the room.

1.

(kitchen)
bedroom
living room

2.

kitchen
bedroom
living room

3.

kitchen
bedroom
living room

4.

kitchen
bedroom
living room

Connect the dots. Write the word.

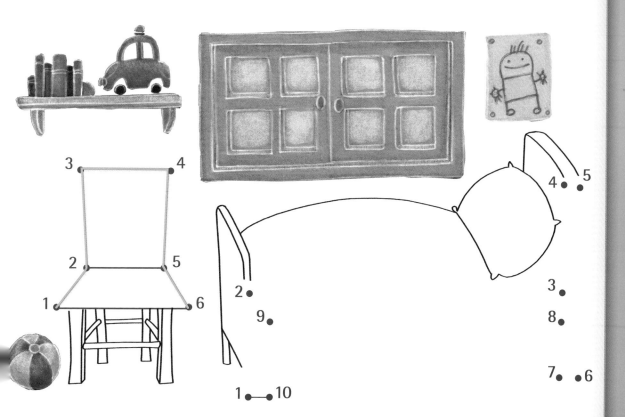

1.   chair

2. _____

Glossary

bears

break

food

run

winter